BOB'S BASICS

PRUNING, TRAINING AND TIDYING

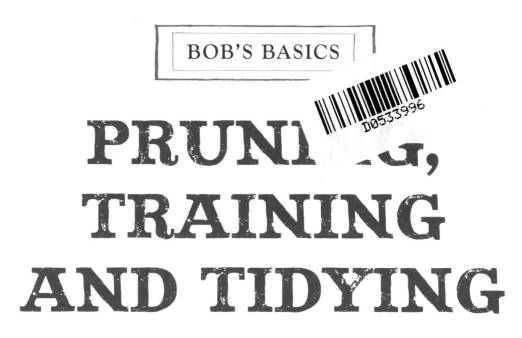

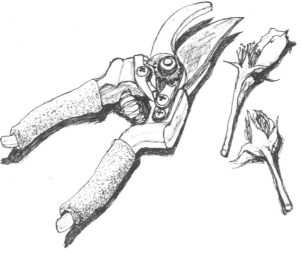

·Bob Flowerdew·

Kyle Cathie Limited

This paperback edition published in Great
Britain in 2018 by Kyle Cathie Limited
Part of Octopus Publishing Group Limited
Carmelite House, 50 Victoria Embankment
London EC4Y 0SZ
www.kylebooks.co.uk

First published in hardback in 2010

Text 2010 © Bob Flowerdew
Design 2010 © Kyle Cathie Limited
Photography 2010 © Peter Cassidy
Illustration 2010 © Alison Clements

ISBN 978-0-85783-470-6

10 9 8 7 6 5 4 3 2 1

A Cataloguing in Publication record for this title
is available from the British Library.

Photography: Peter Cassidy
Illustrations: Alison Clements
Design: Louise Leffler
Project Editor: Sophie Allen
Copy Editor: Helena Caldon

Photographic Acknowledgements:
All photography by Peter Cassidy except
p. 64 by Bob Flowerdew

Printed in China by 1010 Printing Ltd

Contents

Introduction

Most books on pruning, although worthy and well intentioned, are counsels of perfection for the professional gardener, scholars, or growers for show. Rarely is the advice based on what you can leave well alone, nor does it indicate those things you really must do and which are optional.

This book contains the simplest basics you need to know so you can prune those common fruits and ornamentals found in most gardens. Rather than demanding scrupulous attention to 'correct' methods, the following chapters are about how not to prune too much, how to do less pruning, and how to get fair results for the very least pruning, or, put simpler still, it's all about what you can get away with.

Having a garden inevitably involves some pruning. This could be done with little thought, as most shrubs and fruit trees recover fairly well anyway, or it can be done by the book, with you becoming almost obsessive, micro-controlling each plant in tortured bondage. But which book? Merely from curiosity it might be interesting to compare competing methods for just pears, roses, or grapes – any one of which could keep you occupied for life with whole shelves of books devoted to minute permutations.

Right: Espalier pears make the productive ornamental

And therein lies the problem; most of us do not have enough time to learn these highest pruning skills, nor, often, do we start with a clean slate and virgin plants. Most gardeners do not start a garden from scratch but 'inherit' a motley collection of neglected plants from previous incumbents. Few are dedicated specialists wishing to fine-tune a particular plant to perfection or enter their productions in competition. For these specialists there are those countless books and methods to peruse; most gardeners just need to prune plants to keep them confined within their limited space – in the hope that they will still get flowers and fruits, despite their attentions, or lack of.

Time is always short and we may not even know the names of the varieties we are faced with, yet alone their appropriate treatment; of course we would all like to do a proper job, but if that is going to be too hard a task, better we do the next best thing.

To be fair, with generalising, some errors will occur – some plant or the other will not get exactly the best treatment – but even completely inappropriate pruning will rarely kill a plant unless it is repeated over and over again. So this book is about how you can get away with doing the least strenuous, rather than the most perfectionist, pruning.

PS: Although essentially a light job, it's best to prune with a friend – firstly in case of an accident, secondly because the work is easier if one cuts while another disposes of the trash, and thirdly because a second pair of eyes may prevent some glorious mistakes.

Left: The flushes of soft new shoots arising from the horizontal tiers are best simply sheared back once or more times from early summer on

Pruning and

In an ideal world we would not need to prune, but Nature left to itself is not always as we would want it. We certainly must prune away dead and damaged wood to stop it infecting further, and it's reasonable to remove anything looking ugly. We may prune hoping to encourage more prolific flowering or to maintain regular crops of better-quality fruits than we would get otherwise. Large-growing trees and shrubs may need pruning to keep them down to a more appropriate size, especially if we foolishly put them somewhere too small. We may prune plants to certain shapes, for our own reasons, which would not so grow without our interventions; particularly to create flat forms to fit against walls.

training – why?

To do all this we do no more than remove unwanted shoots and train others to our design. Basically, pruning and training is all about redirecting growth – getting the plant to put shoots, leaves, flowers or fruits where we want them. But it's also often a case of squeezing more from less; to fit more plants in an area only big enough for far fewer. Pruning also often compensates for past errors of inadequate planning and inappropriate positioning.

In every case, and for whatever reason, pruning needs to be cunningly performed. For, with all pruning, it's not what you remove that's important but how what you have left will grow back in a few months' time.

Reducing the need for pruning

If you had enough space, you could let every plant reach its natural height and spread in whatever shape it chose to grow. However, often our garden space is very limited and we want to squeeze more plants in than good sense would allow. We then hope to control their growth sufficiently to keep them in that confined space and still get flowers or fruits from them. So, although we want plenty of healthy growth in the early years of a tree or shrub's life, we really do not want it to continue so vigorously forever – particularly as we are then forced to cut off so much surplus growth.

Thus, ensuring plentiful fertility and water are essential initially, but in a plant's mature years it is wiser to be more frugal; the more you feed and water it, the more growth will be made. Of course, competition from everything else will help, and if that is also for light, then be warned: your beloved plants will become lanky and drawn if they are shaded by others. When undertaking pruning, let the light in first; do not prune one or two plants back hard leaving others towering above them, but prune them all down together.

A sure way to reduce the need to prune is to grow choicer, more compact varieties. Many of our best ornamentals are grafted onto rootstocks, which means they will be less rampant than if they were grown from seed and it also keeps them true to type. Most tree fruits are likewise grown on rootstocks to reduce their growth and produce a bigger crop. In almost all situations, the gardener is likely to want the most dwarfing rootstocks, and fortunately these are commonly offered by nurseries and garden centres, so fruit trees now require less pruning than they used to. Of course, you may have 'inherited' older specimens; however, by now their vigour is likely to have reduced and they will not need the heavy formative pruning they required in their youth.

Another way to reduce pruning considerably is through confinement; growing the specimen in a pot, tub or lined hole rather than in the open ground. This severely restricts root growth, thus reducing top growth and pruning and also favours early and prolific flowering and fruiting. This is all gained at the expense of increased watering and feeding requirements – which is a fair exchange with choice fruits and favoured ornamentals.

My main way to reduce pruning is to not do any unless absolutely necessary. It's hard to reduce fruit pruning totally, but many ornamentals can be left for years then cut back really hard and they will recover. True, this is not the perfect approach for all plants, but it works for most!

One other thought – if some plant is creating a lot of competition, needing regular pruning and not repaying you well with flowers or fruit, consider simply digging it out and planting something better...

Above: On dwarf stocks branches and crops grow slowly and remain accessible

Pruning in theory

In theory, the practice and the theory are the same, but in practice we don't find this! There are so many books on specialist ways of pruning this and that, each accompanied by a raft of illustrations of what is to be seen, what is to be done and the expected result. The reality is always at variance, simply because every occasion is different. The soil type, its inherent moisture level, what months the rain predominantly arrives, the shelter, the shade, the feeding, the prevalent pests, the personal history of the plant, its genus, species, even the specific cultivar – all alter the way it will grow and respond to each and every pruning cut. For, as previously explained, it's not what you remove that means the job is done, but how the plant grows back afterwards.

All the variables listed above, and more, affect how each plant responds in general and will produce different results depending on the time of year at which the pruning is done. The specific response also varies with each and every cut made; the more material cut off increases the pressure for shoots to grow back, but it also alters the buds through which it can occur. If small amounts are removed, pruning will have a differing effect than when larger quantities are removed, and different again to a more extreme case. Most truly, pruning is an art not an exact science, yet its essence can be condensed down to some basic principles that apply in most cases.

Left: The trick is in growing the lower branches first

Pruning in winter and in summer

Most of all, what are we after? If it's a flowering shrub we probably want maximum blooms; if it's a productive plant we more likely want bigger, better fruits. The first major factor is timing. It makes a huge difference whether you remove a branch in summer or winter, or indeed, at any time in between. In general, pruning is thought of as winter work and summer pruning is rarely considered anyway. Yet it is this latter pruning that is done during the growing season that has the more value to most gardeners. True, winter pruning helps establish the shape and form of a tree or bush, but this is only in the first years. For the bulk of a plant's life, it's summer pruning that will be more useful for keeping it within bounds and for improving the number, size or quality of flowers or fruits.

Right: Some need little, few need much, but grapevines need pruning more than most else, summer, winter and in between

Pruning in winter

Pruning in winter, when the plant is 'dormant', usually results in the growing back of just as much as was removed. The roots push back so the top rebalances the bottom. Take off a little and a little is added to each shoot; take off much and each shoot grows longer and perhaps other less well-placed buds may also break and shoot. With weak specimens, removing huge amounts can result in the top dying back and the roots withering, but with most healthy subjects heavy pruning results in massive sprouting from hidden buds, as well as from more obvious ones that were deliberately left. (Pollarding and coppicing rely on this last habit, as does the cutting down or laying of a privet or quickthorn hedge – see pages 66 and 93).

When the sap is 'down' (the plant is dormant), most pruning of deciduous plants is about removing firm wood. Cutting back whole branches is considered preferable to lots of snip snipping of smaller stuff – though there is little reason why. Either method takes off a percentage of the flower-come-fruit buds, reducing blooming the following spring, and it also reduces the number of growth buds. The flower-come-fruit buds do not respond much, but growth buds react by growing away more vigorously. Thus, heavily winter-pruned trees soon grow back and, ironically, do not actually come into bloom and fruit as early or as well as untouched ones.

Because there is usually this strong resurgence after winter pruning, this is best for the initial working and training of the frame and shape of the plant. Counter-intuitively, the branches at a given height that you want to grow more strongly have to be cut back much harder than those that have grown well. Those parts that have been cut back hardest push shoots more strongly from the few buds left, thus these grow more vigorously than the many shoots from the greater number of buds that were left on the original, stronger branches.

As plants are dormant in winter it has, rightly, been considered the best time for removing large amounts of unwanted material. It is wrongly, though commonly, held to be also the time to cut back overgrown plants and to restrain their growth. In fact, summer pruning is far more effective for this.

Winter is certainly a less fraught time, when the hours can be found and when pruning is made easier by the leaves being off so you can see what you are doing – and a bonfire at this time of year is fun. However, this is not a good time for pruning all trees; prunus (stone fruit or plum genus) must only be pruned in midsummer. Still, you can always mark the wood in winter for removal later, when the time is more suited. Winter pruning itself can actually commence with the leaf fall in autumn and is often better so done, though evergreens and more tender subjects mostly should wait until spring.

Above: Gooseberries are worth pruning, not just to get fewer bigger berries, but for access to pick. So here you can see last year's shoots being reduced to stubs or spurs on a frame of older wood

Summer pruning

Summer pruning has a different effect – it checks growth. Generally, most summer pruning involves the removal of the ends of young soft shoots, though occasionally whole branches may be removed. Taking away leaves and shoots full of sap reduces the rate of growth, does not cause the immediate replacement of the amount removed, and alters the nature of buds being formed at that time and thereafter. Instead of the shoots extending and ripening more growth buds on their ends, the pruning removes these and the sap then causes remaining buds lower down to become flowering, fruiting ones. Thus, summer pruning tends to increase the percentage of blooms the following year and reduce the total wood these sit on, making a more dense show. This sort of pruning also reduces the current canopy, letting in more light and air and thereby altering the way the fruits and remaining wood ripen.

But, most importantly, as growth is both checked and altered away from yet more growth, summer pruning is a far more effective way to control vigorous plants than winter pruning. One good pruning of three-quarters from each of almost all young shoots keeps a vigorous plant more compact than the same amount cut back in winter. Indeed, repeat several such treatments in the same growing season and you may stunt a vigorous tree. (You can even kill big trees by reducing them to stumps and removing each and every shoot that sprouts).

With most spring- and early summer-flowering shrubs, summer pruning increases the proportion of flower buds for the next spring, making them more floriferous. (Winter pruning would take many buds away, reducing blooming density and encouraging more stem growth.) With fruit trees, summer pruning improves this year's quality and ensures next year's, though additional winter pruning then helps to up the quality of fruits by reducing congested flower buds and thus ensuring fewer, bigger and better-placed fruits.

Because we probably wish to reduce the seriousness of the check caused by removing much material from fruit trees, ideally summer pruning is better done in three or so stages. The first should be done by midsummer, the second around late midsummer and a third later in summer. (If summer pruning is left too late it becomes more like winter pruning, as insufficient time remains before the leaves fall and growth slows.) At each stage, one-third of all shoots, bar the leaders (shoots left to extend the frame), are cut back by half to three-quarters. These

shoots may then be further shortened in winter. Usually these pruned shoots will develop into fruiting spurs along the branches (stubby angular growths that flower and fruit prolifically).

Though, as said before, most pruning is erroneously considered a winter task rather than a summer not only do some plants benefit from pruning at both times of year, but some need even more attention. Grapevines need disbudding (the surplus shoots removed) from early on in late spring and several summer prunings, as well as a winter tidy. I find many soft fruits likewise benefit from shoot thinning in late spring and shoot shortening in early summer. With ornamentals, if the general policy is to shear back hard most flowering shrubs immediately after petal fall, many will effectively be pruned in spring and early summer. So, with deadheading and spring spur removal as well, some pruning can take place throughout the whole year – except for those deepest, darkest days when the bark is frozen, for then the garden is really better left untroubled.

Above: Nipping out competing flower trusses or side-shoots on a grapevine when either is tiny conserves resources for the main flower truss

Pruning is what exactly?

Well, despite some people's claims, not all pruning is best done with a chainsaw – in fact, using a chainsaw is really not recommended. If you actually need one, hire one – and one that comes with someone well insured to use it. But back to the point: the majority of pruning should be done with a pair of clean, sharp secateurs. The old boys and some practised professionals preferred a knife, but secateurs (a French cross between wire cutters and heavy-duty scissors) are easier. Ninety percent of pruning should be cutting off small stuff with secateurs; the bigger loppers, saws and so on are heavier tools that are needed for remedial work on old trees and bushes or the production of firewood.

Essentially, pruning ought to be fine surgery; cutting precise pieces from a plant. The bits trimmed may not always be shoots but may be buds, spurs, roots, or sometimes, as I suggest, almost all the top growth. But most importantly, think before every cut and ask yourself: is it necessary and what will grow back? We need to prune pragmatically for our requirements but also aesthetically, hygienically and, preferably, only when appropriate. Some gardens are ruined by the owner's possession of a new saw and a strong arm! Remember, the ideal pruning should be none or minimal, not the maximum scalping the plants can bear.

Snipping

Snipping should be done using sharp secateurs to cut through shoots. Hold the shoot with the spare hand and apply gentle pressure to bend it so the blade will ease into the cut. Afterwards, dispose of the trimmings sensibly so as to save having to pick them up later; I prefer to drop cuttings straight into a wheelbarrow, trug or cheap dustbin (see page 111 on what to do with this waste). Cut closer to the pivot of the secateurs where there is a more powerful bite, so larger shoots should be pushed further into the jaws, but slender ones may be cut with the blade tips. It's also easier to cut through thick shoots at an angle, not square on.

If a shoot is too thick for easy cutting you should use a saw or sharp loppers. It's claimed to be important to cut upward-pointing shoots, leaving a slope to throw off rainwater – and this may be marginally true. It certainly does make sense to cut back close above a bud, so that this may grow away neatly from the end of the shoot. (Conversely, sometimes you may want to leave a stub if you want to tie in the shoot.) The bigger two-arm secateurs, called loppers, are handy for snipping thicker wood up to finger or thumb thickness, but these are heavier to use. You will need these for renovating old bushes and trees.

Above: Better snip out long spurs or shoots in the wrong place before they get bigger and tougher

'A prune in time saves a lot more effort later.'

Sawing

Sawing should only be done when really necessary – and may involve branches heavy enough to hurt if they fall on you. So always reduce their weight by cutting bits off with loppers first, then tie up the branch to the tree so it will not fall dangerously. Pre-cut a 'V' opposite the position of the final cut so it will break cleanly. For an even neater job, cut off the bulk of the branch some distance away from the tree trunk then, with the weight gone, make the final cut.

It's claimed to be bad to leave snags – stubs of branches lacking buds to regrow. Certainly cutting close to a junction may enable the bark to grow and cover the damage, but if it's slow or fails the exposed wood may rot, spreading to the trunk. I suspect snags are more of an aesthetic problem for the timber trade, who want clean boles, and possibly to those shrubs most prone to coral spot fungus, which rather atypically moves from dead to live wood (see page 87).

Above: A bushman type saw is handy for cutting up, but not ideal for a neat prune

Stopping, tipping and checking

Stopping, tipping and checking is simply using finger and thumbnails to nip out the terminal bud(s) from a green shoot or snipping off the ripening tip of a shoot. Pruned in summer, many buds below the tip will become flower buds; pruned in winter, the buds immediately below may burst later to replace the tip, but, more importantly, other incipient buds further down swell and break, which would not have happened had the dominant tip bud(s) remained. This is one of the most valuable pruning techniques. Removing a whole shoot is an extreme measure; tipping one reduces its growth while retaining most of the buds.

Disbudding

Disbudding is rarely done but is the cleverest form of pruning. Rather than leave a bud to use up resources to make a shoot that you later prune off, the bud is rubbed off in the first place. Often buds come off easiest just as they start to shoot when they become succulent and easily broken. (Removing young shoots on plants, such as grapes, is still called disbudding, for some odd reason.) Completely separately, the lower buds on a cutting or slip that are taken for rooting are usually disbudded or rubbed off to prevent shoots forming from below ground level.

Right: Removing the side-shoots/laterals from a tomato plant redirects resources to the crop

Shearing

Shearing is not the preferred pruning technique; ideally, pruning should be done neatly with skill, foresight and precision but, in practice, many commercial gardeners use hedge trimmers or even brush cutters for summer pruning, and a few do the same for much of the winter pruning. I find shears quick for deadheading most plants and for summer pruning trained fruits, particularly grapevines. Shearing is also appropriate for plants such as lavender, small-leaved hedges (the result does not look good on big leaved ones), topiary and the much-derided but remarkably effective 'lollipop on a stick' pruning of flowering shrubs.

Snapping

Snapping is a technique that some people employ, basically using their fingers to merely snap through small shoots. The argument here is that broken ends heal better than neatly cut ones. This is true of our skin with razor or paper cuts, and beetroot have their leaves twisted off to avoid bleeding, so maybe... Certainly, if you forget to prune grapevines or roses in time then you can pull or snap off their shoots quite cleanly when they're not very long, and the remaining shoots will then soak up the sap, preventing much bleeding.

Above left: I disclaim responsibility for any harm resulting from trying this at home - but it seems that shears are sometimes easier to use reversed from their usual grip...
Right: ...especially in cases such as shearing a ball, or lollipop on a stick

Replenishment or replacement pruning

Replenishment or replacement pruning is a labour-intensive method that is required to optimise crops of peaches, and some other fruits, on a trained tree. Peaches fruit on the (usually shorter) shoots made during the previous summer, and once these have cropped they need to be cut out, or rather cut back, to a suitable replacement new shoot which is then tied in its place. Although straightforward if commenced from a young plant, it is essential to be promptly and repetitively accurate with this type of pruning. I strongly advocate most novices avoid this route.

Remedial pruning

Remedial pruning or repair is simply cutting away growth which just has to go, such as broken or torn branches, diseased material, seriously congested and rubbing shoots, and branches or shoots that are in-growing and will get in the way. All pruning should start with a survey of the plant and removal of such obvious stuff before any other type of pruning is considered. (See also page 43).

Top left: The lower shoot has dieback, which is causing abrasion and congestion and must go
Top right: Surplus suckers from ground level need extricating, and possibly potting up for gift or sale if there's a modicum of root
Bottom left: Remove all figlets from a fig in winter, as any missed get toughened skins and rarely mature
Bottom right: This shoot needs to go, as it rubs on the fence top when weighed down in leaf

Deadheading

Deadheading is a common form of pruning. Blooming takes resources from a tree or shrub, but setting seed is more exhausting. If you deadhead or prune away flowers as the petals fall or fade, this is usually well before the seeds have swollen and so nutrients are saved. The plant can then concentrate all its energy on making more flower buds for the following year, or sometimes for later the same year. If roses are promptly deadheaded or even 'liveheaded' and taken for display in the house, many bushes throw up more blooms. Many other plants will respond in the same way. It's rarely wrong to deadhead ornamentals for this reason, and it also removes a potential hub of disease. On fruiting and seed crop plants, partial deadheading redirects resources to those fruits or seed pods that are left, which then get bigger and ripen sooner. Deadheading is convenient with fingers, scissors, secateurs or shears, depending on the plant.

Deflowering

Deflowering is an even stricter form of pruning than deadheading. This is removing flowers before they set, which is ideal for most fruit- or seed-forming trees and shrubs in their first year, as it prevents them wasting energy and scarce materials making seed until they're well established. If there's any doubt as to variety, leave a few flowers and allow one fruit or two to ripen for identification purposes.

Above: To make this plant a mucg better cropper next year, all flowers are nipped off now
Left: It is almost always a good plan to prune off fading blooms

Defruiting or fruit thinning

Defruiting or fruit thinning is a technique that will prevent biennial bearing (when the tree only crops every other year or so), will up the quality and average size of the fruit borne and will reduce infestations of pests and diseases. It cannot be overemphasized how valuable thinning your fruit can be; it has far more effect on quality than pruning, as such. It's difficult to over-thin or defruit a plant; it is the production of seeds that exhaust the plant, so the less that are retained, the better. If the number of seeds on a plant is reduced by removing half of all fruits, the fruits left behind become bigger, sweeter and better flavoured and will ripen sooner. And, obviously, in the process you remove the misshapen, the damaged, infected and infested, the crowded and badly placed, so the remaining fruits are all well spaced, cleaner and in prime positions. Your harvest will not only be of a far better quality, but you will have fewer, more perfect specimens to eventually pick in place of a host of smaller, poorer ones. Fingers are effective for this kind of pruning, although scissors or secateurs may be better with some plants, such as redcurrants or grapes. With the last the perfectionists will not just thin the number of bunches, but also individually thin the grapes in each as well. (Unless life is too short for such growing for show...)

'It is as difficult to over-thin as to be too rich or too young.'

Left: This one has to go as it would impinge on the nearby stem and is one of a pair, and really, one of those two above my hand ought to go...

De-suckering

De-suckering may need to be done in some cases; many trees and shrubs are grafted onto special rootstocks and these frequently have a suckering habit. Do not just prune these suckers off where they emerge from the ground, as then they will proliferate. Dig down carefully until you discover where they spring from the trunk or root and detach them there as cleanly as possible. Dress the wound before re-covering it. Some trees and shrubs, such as elms, cherries and rhus, are prone to rooting on the surface of the soil or runnering and producing suckers some distance away from the parent. These must be eradicated or a thicket of new plants results.

Left: Shoots from the base of the tree or roots are rarely desirable and need cutting out as hard back as possible

Left: A bit of oomph is needed to cut out older, thicker spurs
Right: I've probably still not been ruthless enough, but there's much less congestion

De-spurring

De-spurring is necessary for some old fruit trees because these, and especially trained apples and pears, become festooned with long spurs (the convoluted stubby stubs upon stubs that build up). These are the bits we want, as they carry the most flower buds and, thus, fruits. However, too many spurs with too many buds on each may be pretty in flower but they are wasteful and will later require burdensome thinning of the excessive number of fruitlets that become set. Congested spurs should be thinned in winter, as regrowth of some new wood is usually sensible, or in summer if vigour still needs containing. Cut each back to the lowest live shoot or fruit bud, then thin these again, if necessary. An unorthodox timing I have successfully employed is thinning the spurs whilst in blossom – you can more easily tell the good from the bad. Also, I remove spurs in summer immediately if they are seen to produce chat fruits – where fruitlets are all smaller than average, wizened or distorted.

Ringing and ring barking

Ringing and ring barking is a hazardous procedure used to reduce excessive vigour. In winter, a ring is cut through the bark nearly all the way round. This reduces vigour, though possibly causes adventitious buds below it to break into growth. Indeed, just making a short cut horizontally into the bark immediately above a bud will often get it to break. Making two partial rings, removing the bark in between and then replacing it upside down and binding it is an approach that is guaranteed to slow down excessive growth, if not kill the plant. Removing, or cutting a complete ring right through the bark around a limb or trunk, especially in summer, can kill most trees. Or rather, kill the top, as the roots or trunk may still shoot again.

However, such a process may be useful when taking out a tree, as pulling off subsequent shoots finishes the job and removes sugars, making the roots less of a prize to honey fungus. (If live roots and/or a stump are left when a tree is cut down they're often the foothold for problems with this fungus. Old dead wood is less problematical.) Ringing has also been performed to single branches just before ripening prize fruits to make them swell and sweeten the more.

Very occasionally, a tree can become bark bound. If one does not grow much for several years its bark may become thick and tight and resist swelling from the inside. This can stop a tree growing. The cure is to run a sharp knife up the trunk, making a vertical slit through to the dead wood. If it is bark bound, the two edges will rapidly pull apart. In any case, coat the wound with the special thick 'paint' available from garden centres to keep the damp and pests out.

Root pruning

Root pruning is hard work but it has great merit. For trees and shrubs growing far too vigorously and not coming into fruit, this technique is done in winter. The whole tree is excavated systematically. Smaller trees may be lifted and replaced, bigger trees have their roots trimmed in situ by a large trench being dug out round the tree. All the roots are sliced through and the cuts on larger ones treated with sealant before they are re-buried. In particular, the tap or main root(s) going straight down into the earth are removed. Some gardeners even replant the tree or bush atop a slab of concrete to prevent the tap root growing back again. Root pruning is often done in two stages over two winters so as not to be such a big shock to the plant.

Renovation pruning

Renovation pruning is the third of the three main sorts of pruning that are usually performed. Initial pruning is done when establishing and training a plant, maintenance pruning during its productive phase, and renovation is for when it has grown past its best. The first is made much of in most pruning manuals but, in practice, is seldom needed by most gardeners (as few are lucky enough to get a blank sheet to plant and train all their own from new). Most gardeners have to maintain trees and shrubs that are already long established – thus the need for simple maintenance pruning. The third case is when plants have gone past their best and need renovating. This will most likely be required after long neglect and when passing into newer hands.

Most old trees and shrubs can be given new vigour, especially if pruning is accompanied by a dose of compost, well-rotted manure and/or wood ashes. It may not be worth resurrecting old blackcurrant bushes, raspberries, or some shrubs, such as daphnes, which resent any pruning, but the vast majority of fruits, trees and shrubs can be renovated or rejuvenated.

In general, they need the dead and diseased wood to be removed first, then the crowded, congested, rubbing and in-growing wood. It may be necessary to thin spurs or shoots to let

Left: This shoot is neither flowering, nor short and close in to the frame, nor needed as there is a good flowering spur in prime condition in a prime spot close by - spot the next to go on the right
Top left: A sea of vertical shoots need cutting away **Top right:** Now only a sufficiency of well budded spurs are left on the horizonal frame

the air and light in again, and they may even need to be cut to the ground and a whole new top resurrected. But don't worry, as I will repeat, unless they're past it anyway, hard pruning in winter will seldom kill plants.

It is the selection and thinning out of the regrowth the following year that is as important as the renovation pruning. For trees, choose the straightest strongest shoot to retain as a new trunk and eliminate all the rest; for shrubs save, say, five shoots. On individual branches thin the new shoots leaving just the best placed. In particular, old but strong trees that have been heavily pruned may develop 'hedgehog' or water sprouts – these are masses of slim vertical shoots which are best removed in summer to prevent them recurring.

Do not be fatalistic about hollowed out trunks and branches – if a tree or branch could fall on you, a building or a passer-by, have it inspected by a qualified tree surgeon. However, strength and vitality lies in the bark layer and thus many hollow old trees can live for decades more productive life.

Bridge repairs

Bridge repairs is a technique that is not exactly pruning, but is too useful to neglect to mention. A very common problem for tree trunks is ring barking by rabbits or deer, where they eat through an entire band of bark one winter, effectively ensuring future death. Cut a few strong young shoots off the tree that are half as long again as the barked area and point their ends to wedge shapes. Next, make T-shaped and inverted T-shaped slots below and above the barked area and a bit closer together than your cut shoots are long. Then gently bend the shoots, pushing their pointed ends into the Ts and in under the bark (still the same way up as when growing on the tree, please). They should hold themselves in place but can be tied with polythene strips and be sealed with pruning compound or clay. These grafts will invariably take as the wood is identical, fresh and desperate to succeed.

Left: Most of the retained spurs are now bursting into flower to later become better spaced fruits

Pruning and training in practice

The theory of pruning takes place in a perfect world devoid of pests and diseases, where a black line on a drawing is a clean cut. In practice, we get cold, wet and dirty: the plant does not match the drawing and that little ink line is replaced by hard work with hand tools.

Think it through carefully before you start pruning – are you sure you need to make this cut? If so, is this the best place, and will anything else get damaged in the process? Many an inadvertent wound is made with the tip of a saw or wandering secateur blade. If it is essential, make the cut neatly and cleanly and paste on a wound treatment if the wound is of any decent size. Remember, this is surgery, so cleanliness, neatness and hygiene are important to prevent diseases entering the wounds and damaging or killing the plant.

There are not many tools that are required for pruning, but a sharp pair of secateurs is essential. A second pair for doing rougher jobs is really handy and keeps the best set pristine. A pair of shears will be useful for many jobs, so get ones that feel comfortable and, to go with them, get a sheet to lay down first to catch the trimmings and make tidying up at the end easier. A pair of loppers (big secateurs with arm-length handles) is handy when removing intermediate-

Right: Rather than keep pruning the life out of these cherries, they're trained down into basket-weave spheroids - unorthodox, but it works

sized stuff of, say, thumb thickness. A proper pruning saw will be needed if you have any old trees or shrubs to renovate; these are designed to cut live wood so they have different teeth from carpenters' saws. The latter makes slow work of green wood and usually cut on push, whilst most pruning saws cut on pull. A bushman saw is designed for cutting lumber not pruning, but it is handy for rougher work. If you have tall shrubs or modest trees, then a long-arm pruner becomes essential. This is 'a pair of secateurs mounted on a very long stick', actuated by a lever.

Solid steps make higher jobs possible but they should only be used to their full with a friend standing on the bottom step for safety! (Many gardening accidents involve steps, so be warned!) Ladders are for professionals and inadvertent suicides. A wheelbarrow is always useful, and a builders' barrow does better for longer than a stylish plastic one. You may also have to burn some prunings, such as the diseased, infected and thorny, and doing so in a steel dustbin with some holes in the bottom, an oil drum similarly prepared, or a commercially made garden incinerator is a safer way of turning prunings to ash than on a bonfire.

Sterilising is vital when pruning. Many bacterial, fungal and viral infections are spread on your tools so, ideally, in between each plant (and certainly between gardens), wipe your blades with methylated or surgical spirit or rubbing alcohol.

Some claim little or no benefit comes from applying commercial pruning compounds or fungicidal paints to pruning wounds, however, generally their trials were done in more hygienic conditions than most backyards. If nothing else, a sealant coat of beeswax, clay, wood paint or proper commercial compound will keep rain and woodworm out for longer and will look neater than bare wounds. With really risky wounds, such as those to prunus outside midsummer when Silver leaf disease may get in, then immediately after cutting cauterise each wound with a blowtorch and paint on sealant. In some sensible countries the effective *Trichoderma virides* paste is still available for use as anti-fungal protection and is recommended, but unfortunately this is not available to amateurs in the UK.

'Safety should be your concern; especially if using sharp tools atop steps, still it's cheaper than the one-way trip to a Swiss clinic...'

Above left: A pair of something like these helps reduce tougher prunings to short manageable lengths brutally easily
Above right: Dirty they may be, but a spray of surgical spirit or methylated spirits, or even duff aftershave (so it does have a use) will kill most pathogens

A note on pruning compounds:

A good read is *A Treatise on the Culture and Management of Fruit Trees* by William Forsyth (1802). Forsyth was given the task of restoring King George III's orchards, and did so way beyond expectation. Forsyth's methods included using his own special compound for healing and sealing tree wounds made from cow dung, lime mortar, wood ashes and river sand, which were beaten to a paste with soft soap and urine. Applied to wounds, this is then dusted with wood ashes and powdered baked bones to dry it. It was claimed to have remarkable effects. I find it works near as well as modern alternatives – although it is not so enduring, is more fiddly to apply and immensely smellier, it does seem to encourage better healing.

Before you start pruning, it really will help if you can readily tell old and new wood apart. Soft green wood and old, rotten, dead wood are easy, but as each species has different bark, on some subjects young and old can be confused unless they are well observed. It also helps to be able to tell growth from flower buds; the former are usually smaller and more pointed, the latter fatter and rounder. Thus, it really is not a bright idea to prune difficult or important plants in dim light, and a sunny day is better. And please wear your glasses if you need them – even if you do not need them, spectacles may save your sight from sharp stems, so wear safety glasses instead.

Performing major surgery is not recommended. Unless you are well experienced, trained and qualified please do not take on any pruning that involves chainsaws or branches that weigh more than you can lift – especially if these are at any height. Particularly beware of anything that cannot safely be got at from the ground or maybe from a solid pair of steps. Pruning small trees and garden shrubs has its dangers, but please do not risk messing with bigger stuff or power tools. Hire a professional, well-insured, mature tree surgeon, preferably one nearing retirement and still with all their fingers...

Above left: The old and dead do not have the same look as the young and healthy. **Above right** A plastic sheet can catch prunings to be easily gathered and disposed of - especially handy with thorny stuff

Where the sap goes, the wood follows

As I keep repeating, pruning is only half the job; next is the training of the resultant growth. As the sap rises in spring, buds come into growth. The highest get the most pressure to grow and nearly always break first, while buds lower down may not break at all because of this apical dominance. This dominance of the highest can be utilised, though, as by bending down branches on a curve we alter which are the highest buds. These buds consequently come into growth when otherwise they would remain dormant.

Trees that are young, vigorous and vertically growing are brought into bearing more effectively by bending their branches down rather than by pruning them. As we bend down branches, their tips cease to grow strongly and they make little more length. The sap, now distributed along their length, causes 'lower' buds to be as high and so also to break and shoot. So, if we need to get, say, a broken, short, espalier limb to lengthen, we temporarily raise the end up as high as achievable so a bud near the top can break and shoot. Once lengthened, lowering it down again causes the sap to be distributed over more buds. With each bud getting less sap they tend to flower and fruit instead of shoot and the limb settles into cropping.

However, we must remember that some growth is necessary. We must therefore always leave a few growth buds, and in turn shoots, in the right places and high enough to sprout and form extensions to the existing framework. It is sensible to choose the central stem of a tree

or the leading shoots of a shrub early on and to leave these leaders unpruned in summer. They may sometimes be tipped back a little in winter, but you must be careful to keep these leaders going, and in the right directions, or your plant's framework will become disjointed. Marking your leading shoots with a twist of coloured wool, paint, or similar can stop you accidentally taking them out.

Above left: Bending a branch over helps buds along it shoot as well as those near the tip
Above right: This cherry has every stem bent down and wound in yet, despite this confusion, it will be mostly the buds on top and outside that will burst

Pruning for training

We can leave a tree or shrub to its own devices and one day it will flower and fruit, given time. That is their nature. However, most do so over a blobby surface of a roughly spherical or ovoid shape. Half this will inevitably be shady, as will the internal volume and, thus, the inside is often devoid of leaves, flowers or fruits and only half the outside is in sun. For a show of flowers this may be fine, indeed those in shade may last longer, but most fruit is better when ripened in the sun.

We need to have two diverse approaches: one for ornamentals where a massive display of blooms is required, and a very different regime for most fruiting plants where we want fewer fruits that are better placed, sweeter and larger. So for fruits, we have devised unnatural forms and shapes in which we grow plants in order to get more of our total crop into the sun. These may also make the plants more accessible for picking, thinning and pest control. However, the plants will always try to recover their 'natural' shape, so we need to prune and train them continually. Fortunately, this becomes much easier once the vigour of the first few years has subsided, so maintenance pruning is less demanding than that needed initially when forming the particular shape.

To turn a sapling into an exquisite espalier, fan, or whatever, is not really that difficult, but as with any manual task, from knitting to dentistry, better results come with practice. So, unless you are really gifted, I suggest you spend a bit more and buy trees that have been ready

Right: Urgent action required, but not much pruning, more training - bending down branches

trained by the nursery – most pruning and training from then on is fairly simple. The more ambitious may try training their own soft fruits, as these are forgiving and quick. However, tree fruits are slow to respond and shape, or replace, and so this is better left to the practised and professional. But have a go if you want and buy or grow a maiden tree – which is a suitable rootstock that has been budded or grafted with your desired variety and grown through its first year. A feathered maiden has lots of side-shoots. If it's a cordon you're after (which is effectively a single branch on its own roots) it's simple: in winter, every shoot, bar the topmost, is cut back to a wee stub with a bud or three on it. But for any other shape you initially need to cut away almost the whole of the top, leaving a tiny stub with a handful of buds at most. Can you be so ruthless? Anyway, you then carefully choose, bend and tie the resultant shoots to make the initial frame of your espalier, goblet, fan, or whatever (see pages 60-64), and from then on the work is the same: in summer, side-shoots (or laterals, as they're called) are shortened, and then, in winter, they are trimmed even further. Meanwhile, the leading tips are encouraged to extend the framework. Not difficult, but fiddly, and precise.

Without doubt, the easier option is to grow whatever you can as a bush on as dwarfing rootstock as is obtainable. Everything else entails far more pruning, though you may feel it is worth it for your favourite fruit.

Standards

These plants are pruned to a clean trunk from the ground up to a given height. Where trees are concerned, a true standard, such as a major orchard tree, has the main branches issuing at just under two metres or about six feet from the ground. Half-standards will spread out from about a metre or three feet up, which enables a mower to be pushed underneath without damaging the foliage. Roses, fuchsias and some other ornamentals are grown as standards, but in their cases, the trunk is kept at about half that of trees, at a metre or three feet or so (and invariably needs a support). Even climbers, such as wisterias have been trained as standards. In each case the top may be left bushy, thinned and tidied, or trained to a goblet or inverted bowl shape.

For large private orchards and arboretums, standards left to their own devices to make bushy tops with just remedial pruning are satisfactory, taking little work and giving huge returns where space is ample. However, where space is limited or higher-quality fruit is desired, more dwarfed and pruned forms are adopted.

Bush

This is the natural shape achieved by most woody plants. Almost all shoots first formed grow to become leaders, branching and filling out in every direction where there is light. Most shrubs have many leaders and form blobby shapes from close to the ground – unless it is shaded. A tree has a short single trunk with a blob on top. Most shrubs can be pruned to a single stem as a trunk, though they may then need extra support to carry the head. Many 'natural' trees can be pruned down early on to make a lower bushy head with no single trunk. However, for our convenience, we mostly give trees a length of clean trunk with low shoots and branches removed for our easier access.

The often derided 'lollipop on a stick' shape is when a tree or shrub is sheared back all over the whole bushy head, preferably just after flowering. This actually works fine for the vast majority of established flowering trees and shrubs, and particularly and controversially for roses (it's much disliked by rose experts), but it's obviously not applicable where fruits are required because you would trim off most fruits at the same time.

Old bush which has been hard pruned, has now grown out again, so these young branches need judicious thinning and tipping, or too much wood will be congested and in the shade

Dwarf bush

Almost all fruit trees are only commonly available on their more dwarfing rootstocks. (Old, big, 'inherited' trees are likely growing on vigorous, much stronger stocks but, by now, have run out of steam and only need remedial pruning and tidying up.) Because of their dwarfing roots, most modern apple and pear trees remain reasonably small; apricots, peaches and cherries too, though plums less so. They're all fruitful if they are just grown as bushes, too. On rich soils, these plants obviously get bigger than on poor but, other than remedial pruning, they can mostly be left untouched. So, in the vast majority of cases, very little pruning has to be done unless you choose to adopt trained forms. If they are grown in pots, they will be restrained and therefore require even less pruning.

Cordons

This is the most restricted form, but the easiest to create and manage – effectively being when one single unbranched stem is grown. Although a cordon really must be summer-pruned, it's relatively simple to do and can be cut with shears. All laterals or side-shoots are pruned back hard to festoon the cordon stem with stubs that form fruiting spurs. (In essence, this is the basis of most fruit pruning, it's just that with some types the branches or limbs are multiple and differently placed.) Although theoretically achievable for almost any woody plant, cordons are commonly created from apple or pear trees and occasionally currants and gooseberries. This is mainly because most fruits grow too strongly to be restricted to 'one branch', but even so, in order to make more varieties more suited, few cordons are grown vertically but are sloped over at about forty or fifty degrees. This makes each longer, i.e. larger, for a given height of its wall or support so that it produces a larger crop and allows strong growers a bit more space. Another way of making strong growers happier, or to get a bigger crop, is to have two or three cordonised branches forming a pitchfork or trident shape. But then it's on the way to being an espalier or fan, or with several it becomes a tidied bush or goblet...

In most cases the leading tip is only lightly winter-pruned, if at all, while all side-shoots are pruned or sheared back at least twice in summer and further tidied with winter pruning. Eventually, the spurs may need thinning on older cordons, though. Because cordons necessarily have weak rootstocks, they always need supports and are best trained against a wall, fence or in a straight row, preferably aligned north–south to get equal amounts of sun on either face.

Above left: Peaches in a tub or large pot need little pruning other than remedially removing diebacked stems
Above right: Hard pruned in winter, these trained apples are also summer pruned ruthlessly with shears

Espalier and step-overs

Espaliers are plants trained into flat forms, like an H on its side, which are well suited to being grown against a wall or fence. As they retain more wood than cordons, espaliers carry larger crops and need greater spacing and less hard pruning to keep them neat. They need good supports, as their limbs are trained horizontally. Again, employed commonly for apples, pears and soft fruits, espaliers can be very decorative with ornamental shrubs but are seldom so seen.

If you are trying to form your own, cut back a maiden very hard the first autumn to get three stubs with three well-placed buds forming three shoots; two are then allowed to grow upwards until they are long enough to be bent down as the bottom limbs the following year or the one after. The middle shoot needs careful stopping and disbudding to get another three buds and shoots that are well placed to form the next pair of limbs. Eventually, four, six or sometimes up to ten limbs are formed, but rarely more as then the highest rob the lower, leaving them crop-less. Once established, summer pruning is essential, when all shoots, other than leaders, are cut back and then trimmed further in winter.

Step-overs are much loved by garden designers but are not often easy to maintain or crop. They are low espaliers with but one tier or one limb trained horizontally above a path or bed edge. Nice idea, though, in practice, they need too much pruning, get in the way, the roots compete when mixed with vegetables and any fruit is shaded by crops and muddied by being low down near a path. Enough said?

Right: And if the winter pruning, spur removal, disbudding, de-shooting and fruit thinning all worked, then we get a spread of fruit over the whole frame

'Pears appear peerless in pairs.'

Fans and herringbones

These are other flat forms for fitting against fences or walls. With a fan, all branches radiate from a single point, or near enough, on the top of a short trunk and each one forks, symmetrically if possible, to fill the wall space. These are straightforward to form; you just need to establish the lowest limbs first. Although most commonly done with apricots or gooseberries, a fan can also be made by the keen pruner using most fruit trees and bushes – especially the less vigorous peaches, plums and cherries.

An apricot or sweet cherry fan, once formed, can be summer pruned with all shoots cut to spurs, save for leaders. Earlier on, the many leaders may be cut back harder in winter to get them to divide. The peaches, sour cherry and some plums need replenishment pruning in late summer, when fruited shoots should be cut away and new ones tied in. Plums were traditionally worked as herringbones, which meant a fan was extended from along the vertical length of the trunk instead of from about one point atop it; indeed, it resembled a fish's backbone and ribs head down in the ground.

Left: Of course, at the end of a row of sloped cordons you'd
have a gap - here's how to utilise it
Centre left: A herringbone does indeed look somewhat like
one - and is effectively a sloping branched espalier
Above: Forming a fan is not difficult, but takes time

Goblet or bowl

This is the principle form for many free-standing fruits, especially dwarf apples, pears, redcurrants and gooseberries, and it is also excellent for showing off roses and other shrubs. The short trunk (it can be tall but it seldom is) is split into five or so main branches that are curved into the shape of a goblet or bowl – radiating out then curving up. Later they will be festooned with spurs, as if each were a cordon. To see what I mean, spread your fingers as if grasping a grapefruit; the shape your fingers form is what we desire for the main branches. Depending on the fruit and scale of the plant, these remain as single branches or, more often, divide into more. (A bowl being flatter and more open than a goblet, which allows more space for branches to divide.)

The goblet and bowl shapes have more live wood exposed to full sun than a solid blob of the same volume. This open middle is vital, so summer pruning is essential, followed by a winter trim and thin. Incidentally, bicycle wheel rims, especially light alloy ones, are excellent for training plants, such as currants, around.

Above: Here is another unorthodox trick - this well formed goblet-come-bowl redcurrant kept producing unwanted shoots in the middle - till I made it dark with the lid

Pyramids, spindles and others

These are all specialised forms for growing fruit (mostly apple and pear), which are created where a single leading shoot is made to form a series of near-horizontal branches, with wider ones at the bottom than the top to allow more sun all over. Although technically simple, it's almost impossible to get it right without loads of practice and I don't recommend any of these shapes. Go on if you want to, but I warrant you'll be happier with bushes or cordons.

L'Arcure

Those curious for such advanced methods will find the Frenchman L'Arcure's work most interesting – shoots are reduced to but one, which is bent down in a curve away from the trunk. A bud and shoot (on top of the curve, of course) as near the trunk as convenient is allowed to grow, with all other laterals cut back during summer. This second shoot is then bent down the other way that winter, and again only one shoot is allowed to spring from near the top of the new curve, and so on. This is a beautiful, if slow, way of covering a fence or wall.

Pollarding, coppicing and stools

These pruning techniques are used more in timber production than the garden, though pollarding is sometimes done for convenience.

Pollarding is an extreme form of the 'lollipop on a stick', with all annual growth cut back extremely hard in winter to a nest of stubs on top of a trunk. The mass of shoots issuing each spring may also be summer pruned by being sheared to a ball or other shape.

Coppicing is when the trunk is removed totally to just a stump so that all shoots spring from ground level. These are conventionally thinned to, say, the best five or so which are allowed to grow on, often trimmed clean, to make poles that will be harvested in five or so years' time.

Stool is the term for a coppiced tree's base, but it is also applied to other plants grown as 'an inverted stool'. Blackcurrants are usually grown as stools, as sometimes are gooseberries, figs, hazelnuts, raspberries and blackberries, and also some thicket forming ornamentals, such as kerria, leycesteria and bamboos.

Above: This mulberry has been pollarded to form a lollipop but has become too big even with winter pruning and summer shearing, so now to repeat the pollarding – believe me this will soon wear a verdant compact sphere once more, honest

Supports

Pruning and training into specific shapes could probably be done without supports, but it would be foolish to do so as without doubt some plants, flowers or crops would be lost. Trees need staking to prevent their roots moving initially whilst establishing; branches and heavily laden tops need supporting to stop them breaking; and most of all, new shoots need bending to our will and tying in place to something while they set. More rigid and substantial is generally better for any support, but it should not be so oversized as to look wrong. Insubstantial is pointless. A dash of black bituminous paint will make different parts, say, trellis, wires, canes and rails, match and look more aesthetically pleasing.

Right: This rubber covered wire is good for temporary ties, but risky for more permanent ones

Posts

These should be substantial and set firmly and deeply so they cannot rock. End posts in rows benefit from an inboard strut, brace or tensioned guy wire. Where softwood posts are used, or even hardwood, make oversized permanent holes in concrete into which replacement posts can be dropped and wedged. This is because the life of trees, brambles and vines far exceeds that of most posts.

Above: Cold but doing its job, metal frames make a s g support

Stakes

These are essential for the short-term fixing of a tree or bush whilst they establish; a vertical stake knocked in first or a diagonal stake fixed afterwards will do if hammered in well. Two stakes planted well on either side, with a cross bar to hold the trunk, make a proper job.

Above: An old bicycle tube makes a functionally, if not aesthetically, acceptable tree tie

Ties and blocks

There is no point doing a good job pruning if all is lost to slow garrotting. Use either proper ties or a soft wide material, such as old tights or bicycle inner tubes – never use wire or plastic string. Check the ties every three months for tightness; if a tie has cut in, extract it where possible then treat the wound before replacing the tie with a softer, looser one. Those compressable blocks on good commercial ties are spacers to be set between the support and trunk or branch to prevent strangling and rubbing. A wad of old cloth or bicycle tube is an acceptable alternative. Clothes pegs make

Left to right: Okay; Awful; Effective; Acceptable; Nasty; Overdone.

great temporary ties for slender shoots, such as peaches and tomatoes.

Wires

These can cause a lot of problems. They do not need to be piano-pitch taut, but only firm and well attached to something not movable. Wires heat in the sun and freeze in the cold, making them unpleasant for young shoots and tender wood. If wires rust, they badly abrade anything rubbing on them. Ideally, cover wires with old plastic hosepipe or use intermediate canes.

Trellis

This is a screen itself and also a supporting frame for climbers. Trellis needs firm fixing to substantial posts before plants are trained to it, as once the plant grows over, it catches a lot of wind. When pruning large valuable plants on old trellis, consider breaking up any damaged sections, extracting them, fixing new trellis in place and then offering back the plant to fix to it.

Intermediate canes

Although often shown in the old diagrams, these are usually, wrongly, ignored nowadays. These come between supporting wires and the plant, reducing damage. The canes are attached to the wires, usually with light gauge wire and often in an attractive pattern, then the shoots are tied to these canes with soft bands of plastic or cloth. Certainly, this is worth adopting with anything valuable, tender or aesthetic, such as a fan apricot.

Air gaps

It's essential to keep a gap between a wall or fence and the plants growing on it so that air can move around. Where stems are tied to canes that are fixed across wires attached to battens only a small gap is created; make this bigger by fitting spacers. If shoots are allowed to fill an air gap, damp may accumulate and rot the fabric, as well as encouraging pests and diseases.

Left: Shame, such a good frame yet so little made of training the tree on it

Frames, arches and pergolas

The life of your plants is probably longer than that of your materials, so build solidly and do everything to ensure durability and replaceability. Do not over-plant and do prune climbers hard so they do not choke out all the light, for then the underside becomes shady, dead and not very interesting. The most common problem is far too vigorous a climber on too small an arch, or whatever; pruning can only help and not cure this.

Left: The trouble with pergolas is that, invariably, growth grows upwards, mostly from the topmost buds
Right: Still, hard pruning can somewhat remedy this, though bottoms will always be gappier than the top

The cast list – pruning by plant type

As I have mentioned before, we need different pruning approaches for ornamentals, where we are after masses of flowers, than for fruits, where we want fewer, bigger, more perfect produce.

Ornamental shrubs

The first general rule with these is, as always, 'if it's not broke, please don't fix it'. Some few specimens, especially conifers and daphnes, simply resent pruning and must not be touched at all, except for emergency remedial work (see List I on page 82). Most deciduous shrubs give their best displays and look finest when left alone, many evergreens even more so. Of course, deadheading is always worthwhile and especially for rhododendrons, azaleas, ericas and callunas.

After flowering is considered the safest time to lightly prune the vast majority of shrubs, as it saves resources being wasted on seeds and helps keep them compact. Trimming off the ends of young shoots at the same time also gives a check, encouraging more flower buds for next year. Generally, with most shrubs you will get away with shears or hedge trimmers. The much-derided 'lollipop on a stick' may result from an overall shearing, but for the vast majority of shrubs this does actually work. Even most winter-flowering shrubs can be pruned after their blooms fade, and even harder than those flowering in warmer months.

Shrubs that flower over many vertical stems, such as ornamental raspberries, leycesteria and kerria, can make better displays if these are thinned in number rather than trimmed back all over. Also, a general trim removes the growing tips, which some shrubs resent and so these respond better to the judicious removal of whole stems or branches in winter. However, both these groups can be allowed to grow and then be cut back hard eventually, if necessary (see Lists 2 and 3 on pages 83-84).

Obviously, shrubs eventually become too big for their position and need reducing. If there are several together, a severe massacre all around is more satisfactory than piecemeal dibbling or, worse, cutting back hard one or two while others are left to tower above. Unless they are old and half-dead the majority of shrubs, such as philadelphus, weigela, forsythia or laurel,

Left: This choisya is a typically tough shrub and can bear hacking back hard to spring afresh

bounce back with a flush of strong young growths and wonderful displays following a severe pruning that removes most of their wood. True, you may lose the odd one, and with others you may lose a year's flowering, but then what a show the following year! (See Lists 2 and 3, pages 83-84).

As we grow ornamentals mostly for their flowers (though some are for foliage), manifestly, if we heavily winter prune, then the less wood and less total bloom there is going to be. However, a few shrubs may be cut down to near ground level each winter or early in spring, mostly multi-stemmed shrubs, such as coloured dogwoods, and really fast growers, such as most buddleias. These can recover to flower the following summer, so they are especially useful in small gardens (see List 4 on page 85).

Some evergreens and most conifers are unable to re-sprout from 'brown' wood, so all cutting back must be restricted to green shoots or bare areas will result. Some evergreens, those grown as hedges for example, are happiest untouched but can be cut down hard to regrow again. Especially difficult to prune well are larger-leaved evergreens, which somehow look odd when pieces are cut away. If frost or wind damages them, dead wood may be pruned out as soon as revealed when growth resumes.

Nearly all climbers are best given enough space to ramble over, then they are at their best just left alone. However, while some, such as akebia, araujia, jasminum (other than *J. nudiflorum*), most honeysuckles and *Solanum crispum*, can usually be left to grow for years, others are just too vigorous and need regular hacking back – especially ornamental grapevines, Russian vine, Boston ivy, some clematis, rambling roses and wisterias. These last half dozen all need hard cutting back regularly before they cover your house or street and have little place in small gardens. As with most deciduous shrubs, the best time for lightly pruning the majority of climbers is just after flowering, or they can be pruned back harder in winter. Clematis fanciers have their own rules for pruning different varieties, but most do pretty well left alone, occasionally sheared lightly after flowering and every so often cut back hard in winter.

Right: Near butchered, this choisya will become a well shaped bush again in a very short time

List 1

These are the shrubs and trees that really are best left unpruned, except for emergency remedial repairs and deadheading. A few specific species may endure treatment but the majority of these genus are best left well alone – in other words, they really resent pruning or are difficult to do well, so don't even consider it!

Almost all conifers, andromeda, aralia, azalea, cercis, daphne, desfontainia, fatshedera, fatsia, garrya, gaultheria, grevillea, hibiscus, kalmia, lithospermum, parrotia, pieris, skimmia, veronica.

List 2

These are shrubs and trees that are better left un-pruned except for emergency remedial repairs and deadheading. If they have grown huge a judicious thinning of whole branches over several winters may be best. A harsh cutting down may result in loss, but most will probably survive. What have you to lose? But to be fair these are difficult to prune well, so perhaps you'd better not do so unless desperate...

Abelia, acacia, aesculus, ailanthus, arbutus, atriplex, azara, callicarpa, callistemon, calycanthus, camellia, carpenteria, caryopteris, ceratostigma, choisya, clerodendron, corylopsis, decaisnea, enkianthus, erica, escallonia, eucryphia, euonymus, genista (other than *G. tinctoria*), halesia, hamamelis, hippophae, hoheria, hydrangea (other than *H. paniculata*), ledum, leptospermum, leucothoe, ligustrum, *Lupinus arboreus*, myrica, myrtus, nandina, olearia, osmanthus, paeonia tree forms, pernettya, phillyrea, phlomis, poncirus, prunus, rhus, robinia, romneya, ruta, salix (as trees), salvia, staphylea, stewartia, stranvaesia, styrax, zenobia.

List 3

These shrubs and trees are better only pruned remedially and deadheaded. A few species may prefer different treatments, but the majority of these are simplest not pruned. If they have grown huge, a desperate cutting down or reworking is unlikely to result in loss but it may be hard to get back a good shape. i.e., these are not easy to prune but are fairly robust and will take abuse; remember, shaping their regrowth is vital.

Acer, amelanchier, arundinaria, aucuba, berberis, buddleja globosa, ceanothus, chimomanthus, cornus (other than *C. alba*, *Sibirica* and *C. stolonifera*), cotoneaster, crataegus (except as hedge), elaegnus, forsythia, *Hypericum calycinum*, ilex (except as hedge), laburnum, lavandula, magnolia, photinia, phyllostachys, pittosporum (unless grown for cutting), potentilla, pyracantha (except as hedge), rhododendron, rosmarinus, ruscus, senecio, syringa, taxus, viburnum.

List 4

These shrubs, climbers and trees can be cut back viciously each winter in order to be confined to smaller places.

Buddleija (other than *B. globosa* or *alternifolia*), some ceanothus hybrids, most cytisus, *Cornus alba*, 'Sibirica' and *C. stolonifera*, eucalyptus, fuchsia, *Genista tinctoria*, *Hydrangea paniculata*, indigofera, *Jasminum nudiflorum*, leycesteria, passiflora, paulonia, rosa, rubus, salix (for stems), sambucus, spiraea (many but not *S. arguta*), tamarix.

Remedial work with most ornamentals

This may be required for ornamentals, regardless of their group, as dead or diseased wood can always appear, storms may break branches or something may fall on or into them (car damage is common). In winter, remove the dead, decaying, rubbing wood; in particular, watch for a common fungal problem of many shrubs, coral spot fungus, which, true to its name, appears as spots of coral-like, pinky, reddy orange. This can move from dead to live wood and must be pruned out and burnt or buried.

Suckers are shoots from below ground that always need removing as soon as they are seen. This is especially true with quality shrubs grafted onto rootstocks where the suckers are often more vigorous and out-compete the desired part. Be careful never to prune away too much of the top or you will encourage the rootstock to grow away.

Reversion occurs where a shrub, say, a variegated or filigree-leaved variety, returns to its original form – unvariegated or entire. These reverted parts must be removed or they take over the whole plant.

Hollow-stemmed shrubs – if these are pruned too far above a node, the tube that is formed can fill with water, freeze, swell and burst the wood. This can progress down a stem. I've never seen it but I guess it's possible, so leave pruning until later, fill the hole with clay, or just prune neatly above a node.

More tender shrubs get some protection from their twigs and pruning them back leaves the remaining wood more at risk so, often, more tender subjects are best left until growth has resumed and when the live stuff can be retained and the dead and unhopeful removed.

Slow growers and Bonsai are best left untouched or very expertly pruned by someone who is practised in the technique. Most shrubs recover and fill out rapidly, so although they may acquire awful-shaped skeletons for winter, they will still be fair in leaf. Slow-growing plants do not recover so quickly, so you will be forced to stare at your errors over several winters before they're mended.

Pruning roses

Probably no area of pruning has given rise to such misleading and excessive practice as pruning roses. Some types of rose are rightly accorded slightly different treatments, but almost every pruning advice is intended 'as if entering blooms in a show', rather than 'for a good display in the garden'. Quite correctly, roses are pruned hard if a few huge blooms are what you want, however, if you want a simpler life, treat roses as tough shrubs; let them grow and bloom then trim them all over to a lollipop with shears after flowering. Only prune them back hard when they're getting far too big or their flowers are held so high you can't see them.

It's worth promptly cutting fading flower trusses off roses where they divide from the single shoot, as then you often get bonus flowering later. Roses are particularly prone to suckering, so any shoots coming from ground level with different-looking leaves to the rest need removing as low down as possible as soon as seen. I advocate heavy mulching after both summer and winter pruning roses to seal down disease spores that might be resting on the soil surface.

The common rose bush, probably a hybrid tea that you inherited in an old bed of several or in a mixed border, is conventionally pruned hard in late winter/early spring, much like a grapevine – that's very hard to a few short stubs of new wood with a couple of buds on each all sitting on a squat stem. This is fine for producing a few big blooms (if you are happy to also feed really heavily, spray against pests and diseases and maybe support those heavy blooms with sticks) but if you're not after a few really monstrous blooms, then do not prune so hard, leave more

Left: Plentiful young shoots betoken a mass of blooms before long

buds on longer stubs and get bigger bushes with many more, albeit slightly smaller, flowers.

When trimming roses, instead of pruning back to short stubs in winter, simply reduce the whole bush all over as if it was a hedge, after flowering and again in winter. Each year the larger number of buds left produce masses of smaller shoots and prolific blooms, often in several flushes. The bush inexorably grows larger so that when it gets too big it can be hard-pruned back close to ground level and started again. This shearing method is especially useful for most old-fashioned roses which otherwise make huge clumps of somewhat twiggy growth.

If you want an amazing display but more work, try creating swags and splaying. You need to prune back hard to get a few strong long shoots, and then the next winter do not prune these back but only trim them, then bend them down until they are almost horizontal or encircle a post in a squat spiral. New shoots will burst out all along them with masses and masses of blooms. Now you can cut these spent shoots out after flowering whilst schooling another set for bending down that winter, or you can just shear back the young shoots and retain the old stems for several years of blooming before replacing them. Sometimes shoots can be held out horizontally and left looser, just tied at the ends to make sagging curves, or swags, which become laden with short flowering shoots and are very floriferous.

Rather than pruning out much of the wood in winter, causing unwanted resurgence, all the stems can be trimmed and then woven back into and amongst the others to plait or weave an inverted 'basket'. Although much more time-consuming, the retention of so much wood gives large numbers of blooms on short stems (which are sheared off as they fade). Initially, three to five shoots should be bent down and tied in as tightly as possible, then all summer stronger shoots should be bent down and woven through and in winter the smaller ones as well. The interior becomes shady, fills with dead wood and is a haven for wildlife. Eventually it becomes unwieldy so, after several years, the 'basket' is finally removed one winter with all the weak and dead shoots. The strongest shoots are shortened back to just a few buds that form new strong shoots in spring, then the same process is carried through again.

Let alone and recovery is the best advice – remember the best pruning of all is none. If each rose is left alone, other than deadheading-come-shearing in summer, it becomes big, flowering profusely. However, if space is limited, soon that limit is reached.

Fortunately, most varieties are capable of regrowing if you chop them down near completely in winter. Well, preferably to three or five strong younger stems. For bushes, these can be very short – you may lose a year but some unseen buds will usually erupt, even if you've left only old wood and no younger.

For climbers, these are mostly strong-growing, ordinary roses that you want to climb over supports, so young stems can be left untrimmed. With ramblers, though, which have incredible vigour, I'd recommend cutting everything to the ground then ruthlessly selecting just a few of the young shoots. These can be let go until entirely overgrown again and cut back after so many years. But ramblers are so vigorous they're only sensible in small gardens if they are treated much like raspberries, with every shoot older than a year cut back to near the ground in winter.

Remember, if you feed and water them well for the year after, very few roses (or most other shrubs) will be killed off by a hard cutting back in winter, unless they were old and worn out.

Above: Removing lower side-shoots, leaving only those near the tips, encourages most new growth and bloom higher up for reluctant climbers

Hedges and topiary

This is pruning work that must not be avoided. Hedges need very severe cutting back in their first few years to get cover all over. Once established, they need shearing rather than pruning. However, large-leaved ones, such as cherry laurel should have individual stems pruned neatly with secateurs so as not to have dead half leaves decorating the finish. I use powered hedge trimmers on commercial jobs but I do not recommend them for domestic use and much prefer using shears. The work is slower, but less noisy, less dangerous and less tiring – and may look better.

Put down sheets to collect the trimmings, then start by trimming the sides first, then the top. Solid secure steps are useful even for fairly low hedges. Formal hedges should not have a rectangular cross-section but be slightly wedge-shaped; narrower at the top than the bottom. A tight bit of fishing line makes a good guide, a builder's laser level is even better.

It's best not to cut hedges from early spring until midsummer, as this disturbs birds nesting. Cutting regimes vary; for optimum neatness small ornamental hedges too small for bird nests, such as box or rosemary, may be trimmed three or even more times through spring and summer. More frequent cuts are better but, for convenience, most barrier hedges can be done but once, usually in winter; beech and hornbeam retain their leaves so should be left until spring. Some, especially leylandii and similar conifers, are better sheared in late summer. Informal hedges (not neatly uniform, often mixed flowering shrubs) are left until they need reworking or are trimmed back after flowering. Wildlife hedges should be trimmed in winter once the berries have all gone. Special care needs to be taken with coniferous hedges, as if they are ever cut back too hard and expose brown patches, they will never recover, thus these

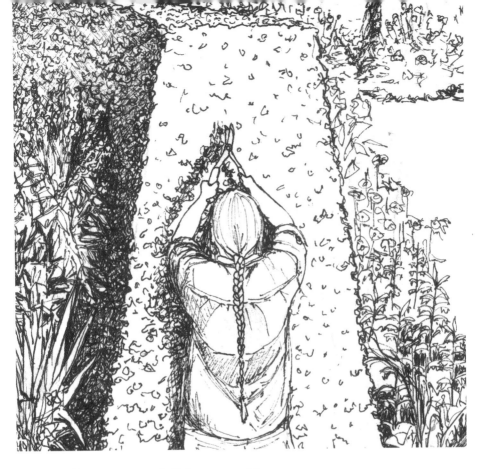

are impossible to get neat again if they are ever let go.

Cutting down, i.e. removing all the top growth to stumps when old and scrappy, rejuvenates hedges such as quickthorn (crataegus), privet, yew, box and laurel. Indeed, almost all common hedges, other than conifers, and many shrubs, can be cut down to near ground level in winter and will re-sprout and form a new neat hedge quickly. Afterwards, you should trim them in summer and cut back hard in winter to rebuild a dense hedge. Laying is when the old scrappy hedge is reduced to the strongest stems, each half cut through near ground level, bent down and interwoven with each other and/or stakes. This makes a stock-proof hedge quickly and bridges gaps far better than simply cutting it down.

Above: Cutting a formal hedge is slow using such short shears...

Productive garden pruning

This is where it really pays to prune properly and carefully. Although most ornamentals are best neglected, most fruits need some pruning annually. We may prune to correct problems, such as biennial bearing (see page 96) but, generally, we prune to stop trained forms growing congested. Here we are not after the maximum number of flowers, but we want larger, cleaner, sweeter, better-ripened fruits. Fortunately, a low-prune policy can still be applied to many fruits by growing them as bushes.

Left: A long spur needs trimming back, the others are too congested still, and the branch is set too close to the wall

Tree fruits

Stone fruits are treated much the same as their ornamental cousins – they are best left almost untouched. Their pruning is not always simple if they're to be trained, their stocks are not very dwarfing and they are prone to a wound entry disease called Silver leaf, which means they should never be pruned except, if necessary, in midsummer. Any winter damage needs repairing and patching instantly. Cherries and peaches have been trained as fans, and plums as herringbones (see page 62), however, these are then so arduous to maintain that I strongly recommend against this. Instead, grow them on the most dwarfing stocks offered as free-standing bushes, or in containers and only remedially prune them when strictly necessary.

Morello sour cherries are different to sweet cherries and can be pruned harder, or rather can have their twiggy shoots thinned ruthlessly. Bonanza and other Peento (flat) peaches are especially dwarf growing and are recommended as they need minimal pruning. Apricots are good as bushes and are not difficult to maintain as fans as they are more spur forming, though frequently many died-back shoots do need removing.

Although mulberries can be pollarded with ease if troublesome, they are usually best as bush trees. Be warned, they get big. Walnuts and sweet chestnuts are also better left untouched, except for strictly necessary repairs, as they heal poorly. Hazel, cob and filbert nuts can be treated very hard; they're often coppiced for use as poles. When grown for their crop they were traditionally trained as huge wheels, but now they are sensibly grown as stools with five or so almost vertical main 'branches'. In winter, strong-growing unwanted vertical shoots and strong side-shoots must be cut out as well as the often-prolific suckers. New, dwarfer varieties are more suitable for the garden than older larger sorts.

Figs are best confined to tubs, reducing pruning to a minimum, as this keeps them down to size and promotes cropping. In the ground, and even against a wall, they relentlessly become bigger, even when confined with a brick compartment, and worse if they find moisture or food. Never, ever feed or water near fig trees! They can be trained but are usually left to form a bush or stool. Longer jointed shoots are unproductive and can be removed leaving the more fruitful, short-jointed wood. Once growth starts, figs bleed with caustic sap that will possibly congeal with heat, but it is better to prune before this happens, preferably by late winter. If all small figs are not removed or protected in early winter, some endure only to swell and drop later, robbing the rightful main crop.

Apples, pears, quinces and medlars are simplest grown as bush trees that are only remedially pruned. Modern dwarfing stocks keep these much more compact and manageable, though they always need support. When trained, most apples are pruned to spurs on a framework, usually cordon or sometimes espalier. Then they need summer pruning (shearing) of all shoots, except leaders and a further winter tidy to shorten the leaders and reduce spur numbers. Pears are more amenable than apples to similar training, which is fortunate as the best prefer growing against warm walls. Quinces and medlars are always grown as bush trees on short trunks and only remedially pruned, though, in theory, they could be trained. The Japanese quince, not Cydonia but Chaenomeles, is unruly, makes a dense hedge and is one of the least trainable of plants.

Tip bearers

Some apple varieties are tip bearers, which means they do not form spurs easily and fruit upon the ends of last year's growth. This is inconvenient as these would be pruned off by summer or winter pruning, so they should rarely be pruned! Oddly, most tip bearers are early varieties; it is best to grow them as dwarf bushes with an occasional thinning of congested shoots every few years. 'Discovery' is one of the better earlies; it is prone to tip bearing but also spurs.

Biennial bearing

Some apple trees are determined to throw huge crops, which are then all small, less usable fruits. The following year, the exhausted tree bears few flowers or fruit as it's forced to take a year off to recover. By reducing the number of spurs, and by thinning the fruitlets, the total crop is reduced in number so the remaining fruits get bigger, the lesser number of seeds alleviates the plant's exhaustion and the tree returns to regular bearing.

Above: Grow fruit in tubs and, preferably, on dwarfing stock
and you will rarely need to do much pruning

Soft fruits

These need pruning more than tree fruits but can usually be recovered more easily, even if they are neglected for a while. I have often left raspberries and blackberries unpruned for several years to little detriment other than the brambles get too big for their allocated space. (New bramble canes can simply be tied back onto and over the older ones.)

Blackberries

The blackberry tribe, including hybrids such as loganberries, crop on side-shoots from the canes that grew the previous year. True blackberries may fruit yet again in their third year but, by then, the canes are stiff and infested with troubles, so they are better replaced than retained. Once fruiting has ceased, all old canes should be removed (cut them into arm's-length bits and bundled up for disposal as you go or you will be trapped), while the new ones are tied in, and may be shortened for convenience. Strong supports are needed for these, as some are large, vigorous plants that need to be five paces apart or so. They live for a very long time. As new canes emerge between the old, they need holding out of the way until the old ones are cleared. I find large rubber bands made from bicycle inner tubes with 'S' hooks perfect for this. Some train each year's canes in opposite directions along a row to keep them apart, but this isn't necessary. Some hybrids, such as boysenberry, seem more miffy and resent being tied to wires without cane intermediaries.

Raspberries

Most raspberries fruit in summer on canes grown the year before, but some crop in autumn on the canes grown that summer. For the latter, all canes should be reduced to ground level in midwinter and emerging new canes should be thinned to a hand's width apart or more. These may need confining between strings or tied to one strong wire to stop them flopping over. As these are shortlived, they can be held directly by wires.

Those raspberries that fruit in summer, on canes that grew the previous year should be thinned as they emerge and may be tipped during late summer to encourage fruiting side-shoots that can be tied in. Once fruiting has finished, old canes should cut out at ground level and new ones tied in their place. With summer fruiters, there are old and new canes standing together in summer, so if they are very vigorous they may need more thinning than autumn fruiters. Either type will form runners underground and move away from their allotted spot. After a decade, raspberries will probably be virus-infected and need replacing.

Left: Raspberries need their canes well spaced
Right: And use light supports to stop them flopping

Blackcurrants

Blackcurrants are grown as stools with many shoots coming from the ground. They crop only on young shoots grown the prior year – annoyingly, with most sprouting from existing canes. Thus, pruning to remove old canes removes the young ones too. So regard the stool from above and, over three years, remove all old stems to near ground level in one-third segments (like fat slices of cake). Young shoots emerging from near the ground can be left but anything older must be cut out, and this is best done when harvesting. Indeed, the stems with crop on can be carried somewhere more comfortable for picking. The bushes are seldom worth keeping beyond a decade, as they inevitably succumb to virus problems. Be not afraid to prune viciously – the plant will bear fewer, bigger, richer berries.

Red and Whitecurrants

Red- and whitecurrants are completely different to blackcurrants as these fruit on wood that grew the previous year, but also on spurs. Summer prune, with shears, and do so early, then tidy up further in winter, or leave more young wood for bigger, sourer crops. Often grown as goblets or bowls on a short leg, these plants are easily trained as cordons, espaliers or any other form you imagine and will crop anywhere, even on shady walls. Although the tops get old and fail, new shoots from low down can be trained in as replacements and the plants will go on indefinitely. As these are so forgiving, quick and responsive, and the basic method for them is the same as for most apples and other fruits, they are good to practise on. Again, be not afraid to prune viciously!

Right: Blackcurrants are best pruned viciously hard, leaving only the strongest and youngest

Blueberries

Blueberries fall into three groups: high bush, low bush and rabbit eye, which are, theoretically, treated quite differently. However, we mostly have hybrids, and as these are usually grown in containers of ericaceous compost, they are effectively dwarfed. Pruning then consists of removing congested, old and twiggy stems while training stronger younger shoots into good positions. These can over-crop themselves, so pruning out spare wood does no harm.

Above and right: Blueberries only need the old and congested, dead and twiggy wood removing

Gooseberries

Gooseberries were once grown as stools, which meant picking the fruit gingerly; they are better as hard-pruned, wide-open bowls of five branches on a short leg, but they also make good cordons, espaliers and fans. The main branches become festooned with spurs after hard pruning in both summer and winter (often done very late in winter to avoid birds eating the buds) just as for redcurrants. Plant them a pace or two apart and expect to lose them sometime after a dozen years, so take cuttings before then.

Kiwis

Kiwis are rampant climbers that are only happiest when clambering over trees; in this situation, if you have both male and female plants, you get loads of fruits. Pruning is only remedial; however, I have seen them made into (huge) espaliers hard-pruned back to spurs so, amazingly, it can be done.

Above: Gooseberries need ruthless cutting of last year's shoots to one or two buds, usually before, during and after winter

Grapes

Grapes desperately need the most ruthless pruning, and these have more methods than are credible. This is essential pruning you can't forget as they grow too vigorously to ever go unpruned (covering trees in two seasons) and then disastrously produce too much fruit that fails to ripen. The skill with grapevines is being brutal; once a vine is established it's reluctant to die and fruits better the more viciously pruned it is in winter, spring and summer. Vines only fruit on shoots coming from buds made on wood grown the year before. The more you leave, the more bunches you get but the later they ripen, if at all. Prune hard to get fewer, better bunches. For table fruits you should without doubt grow vines in tubs, and, even better, bring those under cover in late winter for earlier protected crops.

Above left: Tubs allow more variety in the same space by constricting growth
Above right: Hard-prune all young grapevine shoots to one or two buds

Vines in tubs

Growing grapes this way seriously controls their vigour and allows you to plant more varieties in a limited space. Grow one vine per tub up a stout pole to head height and tip it once it reaches the top, then tie in and tip all side-shoots. In winter, cut off all of the new growth leaving but one stub of young wood with three good buds. Allow three shoots to grow in spring then tie them up the pole, remove the flower trusses and tip them once they reach the top. In the third winter, reduce the three shoots to three stubs with two buds each. From these six buds shoots will grow in spring, and once flower trusses have formed on these, choose the three best shoots to carry fruit, cutting off the others at three leaves to reduce the first year's crop (though in future years all six shoots with their flowering trusses can be retained). Tie the selected shoots to the pole then tip the tops and side-shoots as before. Each winter, cut back to three or four stubs of new wood, each with two buds. The spurs these stubs form slowly become thick arms and a strong bud appearing lower down can be allowed to shoot and become a replacement for this old 'head'. Otherwise, all buds appearing from old wood should be rubbed off as they are unfruitful.

Vines on wires

Vines planted in the open ground or on low walls need wires, strong ones. I prefer to use two wires: one at knee height to carry the canes, and another at elbow height to fasten the tips of the year's canes to and to support anti-bird nets. The first year's pruning is exactly the same as for a tub, with one shoot cut back hard. This is reduced to three buds, of which the two best shoots in spring are trained each way along the wire and tipped at a couple of paces both ways, with any flower trusses and side-shoots removed. In winter, these are left and the next spring these canes make shoots from buds at most joints. Those bearing flower trusses are left unpruned and when they reach the top wire they are tied in and tipped. (Later that summer, optionally with shears, everything that rises above the second wire should be cut off.) All non-fruiting shoots should be reduced to three leaves, and so should any excess fruiting canes; remove the surplus ruthlessly. The first crop should be no more than a half dozen bunches, later ones can be much more. In autumn, all the shoots rising from the two oldest

canes, now rods, should be cut down to stubs with two buds. In spring, these will shoot and those in the best positions should be thinned by about half. Thus, as this is repeated every year, the permanent horizontal rods build up spurs and when these become unwieldy the whole rod can be replaced by a new strong shoot from lower down.

Vines under glass and on high walls

The rod and spur system is again the better choice here, however, there is the problem of position to contend with. In a small greenhouse, you can only run the rod along the eaves and train the shoots up wires under the glass, but they tend to be held too close to it, so make sure you allow a big air gap! In bigger greenhouses, an error could be planting along the front with the rods running up inside the front wall and back under the roof. The result would be most growth and fruit comes from the tops as little gets made lower down. It's better to position the rods so each vine's fruiting canes run at the same level; i.e. one vine provides a rod running along the top third of the roof, another a rod running along the middle third, another one in the eaves and a fourth along the lower front wall. Each builds up spurs along the horizontal section to provide shoots annually which are trained to the next wire up, so each variety produces bunches along the length of the house. Likewise, on a high wall do not train one vine to cover it, though it would do so happily. Instead plant two or three so that each forms its horizontal rod at a different level across the wall. Again, the annual shoots are tied to the next wire up, tipped, then pruned back to spurs again in winter.

Tidying by pruning

Tidying and trimming the herbaceous bed is barely considered pruning, but to most intents it is: the same principles are involved of removing unwanted pieces and redirecting growth. First of all, many herbaceous plants, flowering and cropping, can benefit from having their young shoots thinned. You get fewer, but better spires of plants, such as delphiniums, if you limit the number of shoots per clump. Potatoes produce much the same weight of crop from five stem haulms as three, but the three have fewer, bigger tubers that are better for baking and chipping.

More akin to real pruning is the revoltingly named 'Chelsea chop'. At the time of the RHS Chelsea Flower Show, on the cusp of spring and summer, you cut back hard young shoots of most later-blooming herbaceous plants, delaying their flowering and producing a better, more multi-headed show. Deadheading spent flowers where seeds or fruits are not wanted makes sense for herbaceous plants as for shrubs, as nutrients are saved for growth and flowering. The herbaceous tribe also need an autumn trim to tidy up their decayed leaves or stems; some, such as hemerocallis, almost disappear, leaving a neat crown, but many leave a thicket of died-back stems. Traditionally these were pruned off at ground level for neatness, however, it is better to prune them off at a hand's width from the ground as the stubs protect the crown, catching leaves and soil, and also mark the crown in case of snow or for when applying mulch. Herbaceous trimmings are mostly thin and soft enough to be added to the compost, though they can be bundled into wildlife nests.

Right: Short-lived perennials, such as wallflowers, live longer and flower better the following year if promptly deadheaded

What to do with the waste

Some of the longer, straighter prunings can be used in place of garden canes around the garden; they can be used straightaway or are stiffer and last longer if they are thoroughly dried first. Other bushier prunings may be handy for pea, bean and sweet pea sticks. Birch twigs and similar can be made into besom brooms.

All smaller and greener stuff can go into the compost bin, though ideally they should be shredded or at least chopped first. Some thorny prunings that are nasty to handle can be burnt, but a neat use is to cut them into, say, arm lengths, tie them into tight bundles (lay strings on the ground as parallel lines then lay prunings across them, pull them together and tie strings without ever handling the thorny stuff) which can be secreted into dead spaces in evergreens, conifers and hedges to become wildlife sanctuaries.

Of course, bigger prunings can be chopped into short lengths for kindling, though round stuff does not catch as well as split. Any sawn wood should be reserved for someone's wood stove or fire, especially that from fruit trees, which have delicious smoke. Why not sell them by the gate for charity come Christmas?

Lastly there is the bonfire – preferably this should be a small metal incinerator, but if you must burn then dry the stuff first. Build a stack, then feed this piecemeal into a garden incinerator (a steel dustbin or oil drum with holes in the bottom stood on bricks does well), or on to a small fierce fire built up on metal rails on bricks so air can get underneath. Do not simply build a stack and burn it once dry as you incinerate all critters hiding inside, not just bugs but bigger ones. Make your fire over clean ground – preferably covered with a metal sheet so that you can gather the wood ashes. (Those from burnt prunings are reckoned far more valuable sources of potash and other elements than firewood ashes from logs. Keep dry and, if not needed elsewhere, spread under fruit trees in spring, especially cooking apples and gooseberries.)

So in a nutshell, do not be afraid to prune – you will rarely kill a plant and, with ornamental shrubs, a brutal cutting to the ground in winter will result in an amazingly rejuvenated plant and a staggering display in a year or two. When it comes to fruit trees, they are mostly best left alone, but most soft fruits can be pruned hard in winter and/or summer and are good to practise on; and if you have grapevines, prune them utterly ruthlessly almost as if you hate them and you'll not go far wrong.

Index